CONTENTS

INTRODUCTION

Any nonprofit organisation owes it to itself to engage in creative and enthusiastic fundraising activities in order to be able to fund the activities it was formed to undertake, recognising that there will always be potentially enthusiastic supporters amongst its various constituencies.

All too often, however organisations fail to realise this potential and therefore fail to fully deliver on their charter or objectives. The reasons for this failure are primarily twofold (assuming all the while that the cause or organisation is legitimate and worthy): failure to ask for support and failure to adequately prepare for that "ask."

Elsewhere in this series of Quick*Guides* 'making the ask' is explored in some detail. This Guide examines the various steps that are necessary to ensure thorough preparation for that eventual request for support.

Preparation for Fundraising will take the reader sequentially through those areas that need to be addressed prior to approaching potential donors, from review of the constituency to staffing and training considerations. It also reviews some of the tools an organisation needs to have at hand, including tax benefits and the prospect of international fundraising. Finally, the concept, process and attributes of developing a fundraising strategic plan are briefly explored.

All organisations have a range of constituencies, each of which will be supportive depending on the relevance of the organisation to them and the extent to which they are cultivated. They include, but are not confined to:

- Clients and their families (such as in hospitals)
- Current, past and future parents and alumni in schools and universities as well as staff
- Corporate supporters
- Trusts and foundations
- Suppliers
- Neighbours
- The catch-all category of "friends" of the organisation who just have an interest in the activities of the organisation.

Reviewer's Comment
Whilst they are not your priority, it's also good to have your eye on a couple of "long shots" – i.e., potential donors who do not have a known affiliation with your organisation but who, according to your research, are wealthy and philanthropic and have a proven interest in your cause.

The challenge in most organisations is to cast the net as widely as possible, identifying, recognising and addressing the different giving motivations of the different groups.

FRIEND RAISING AND DONOR CULTIVATION

As a prominent and successful fundraising executive once said, "I never ask for a gift from anyone who is not already a friend." Whilst it clearly is not possible to actually befriend all potential supporters, it is possible to allow them time to become acquainted, or reacquainted, with the organisation before suggesting they give to it. This process might be as simple as ensuring that constituents receive the regular publications of the organisation. But in the case of potential major-gift donors, it will desirably mean face-to-face cultivation meetings with senior staff and key volunteers. The more substantial the potential outcome, the more tailored, personalised and intense the cultivation needs to be.

Potential donors are generally assaulted from all sides by worthy causes, and the challenge is to gain the attention and interest of the potential funder.

At the lower or more general end of the giving scale, there is no substitute for providing project information that includes rationale, timeline and anticipated outcomes.

Reviewer's Comment
Some potential donors you want to reach might not be acquainted with your organisation or the specific project. Unless you can unearth some connection with them through your contacts, the best way to rectify this is by inviting them to an event where they can be informed about the cause and introduced to the CEO and other key individuals.

A key mistake is to ask for a gift too soon. The vital processes of cultivation will not only increase the propensity of the potential donor to give but will also impact substantially on the likely quantum of the gift. It is sometimes prudent, therefore, to deliberately hold back on an "ask" until not only the project is right but also the time is right.

Planning for key asks is a natural consequence of vigorous and detailed donor research – one relies on the other.

QuickGUIDES
everything you need to know...fast

Preparation for Fundraising

by Frank Opray

reviewed by Alison Woolley

WIREMILL
PUBLISHING LTD

Across the world the organizations and institutions that fundraise to finance their work are referred to in many different ways. They are charities, non-profits or not-for-profit organizations, non-governmental organizations (NGOs), voluntary organizations, academic institutions, agencies, etc. For ease of reading, we have used the term Nonprofit Organization, Organization or NPO as an umbrella term throughout the *Quick*Guide series. We have also used the spellings and punctuation used by the author.

Published by
Wiremill Publishing Ltd.
Edenbridge, Kent TN8 5PS, UK
info@wiremillpublishing.com
www.wiremillpublishing.com
www.quickguidesonline.com

British Library Cataloguing in Publication Data
A catalogue record for this book is available from the British Library.

ISBN Number 1-905053-15-0

Printed by Rhythm Consolidated Berhad, Malaysia
Cover Design by Jennie de Lima and Edward Way
Design by Colin Woodman Design

Disclaimer of Liability
The author, reviewer and publisher shall have neither liability nor responsibility to any person or entity with respect to any loss or damage caused or alleged to be caused directly or indirectly by the information contained in this book. While the book is as accurate as possible, there may be errors, omissions or inaccuracies.

I dentifying specific donors is a crucial part of the fundraising process. Some may already be on the organisation's database because they have given previously. Others may be identified because they are part of the constituency of the organisation as discussed previously, or they are part of the general philanthropic community and have expressed interest in the type of activities in which the organisation engages.

Increasingly, the fundraising endeavours of nonprofit organisations are focussing on fewer and larger gifts coming from an ever smaller proportion of the various constituent bodies. By concentrating on those who are able to give large gifts, the fundraising effort can be substantially more effective and efficient.

The corollary of this is that identification and cultivation of potential major donors takes on increased significance, as does the emphasis which needs to be given to donor research.

Reviewer's Comment
It is best to cover both ends of the spectrum: The lower-level annual-giving programme can always be ticking over, providing steady reliable income and acting as a means of informing a wide audience of your mission, needs, aims, vision and successes. It is also useful as a pipeline, "feeding" those donors who have been particularly generous, steady and loyal into your major donor prospect pool.

Research is a crucial initial component of identifying and recruiting potential donors. Not only will it help determine whether a potential supporter can be converted into an actual supporter but it can help determine whether a potential supporter will be a substantial donor or not.

The process of research tends to be a combination of searching the public record; identifying where else the prospect might have given and for what causes; examining past giving habits within the organisation itself; and talking discreetly with knowledgeable but confidential observers. The results

Continues on next page

should uncover likely giving interests and passions (the so-called **"hot buttons"**), key relationships (business and social), and likely interest in naming opportunities or other forms of recognition. Along the way, the researcher will also be seeking to identify who amongst the organisation's key volunteer askers will be the most appropriate person to make the ask. Needless to say, extreme confidentiality is required at all times.

As the research proceeds, one eye will always be on the contingency of just "when" it's the right time to ask, noting that it is often wise to wait until full research has been done.

"How many potential major donors should we have?" This is an often-asked question. Successful organisations generally work on that four candidates will be required for each major gift received. The success of most major capital campaigns turns on the ten or so prime gifts received therefore, in preparing for a campaign,

much time will be spent identifying, researching and cultivating the 40 most likely candidates, largely to the exclusion of all others during the early phases of a campaign.

Ongoing fundraising activities will also benefit from research. Whole new constituents may be identified as may different approaches that will be useful when applied to current constituents.

Reviewer's Comment
Keeping rigorous tabs on all your potential donors and their contacts, interests and individualised cultivation plans is vital. Bespoke fundraising databases are powerful tools to help store, analyse, recall and present information, but they are expensive. In their absence you should develop simple information-management tools, such as tables, to give an overview of your prospects and the "next actions" that are needed.

An absolutely crucial feature of successful fundraising planning is to have projects that stem from a well-thought through, board-adopted, strategic plan which looks forward at least ten years. This plan will include facility needs based on the philosophy and mission of the organisation and its projected structure and size.

Reviewer's Comment

The case for support – possibly translated into individual projects – should represent real needs of the organisation, as articulated by its leadership. There should be full buy-in and support of the vision before fundraising starts so that the development function has the mandate to move forward on behalf of the organisation and can convey passion and belief to potential donors.

From a donor engagement standpoint, successful fundraising organisations are alert to the need to:

■ Communicate to potential donors that the philanthropic needs relate directly to the long-term strategic goals of the organisation.

■ Provide choice to donors, recognising that different candidates will have different giving motivations.

A prudent approach prior to embarking on an appeal for a specific project is to conduct a fundraising feasibility study. This will not only help quantify the amount that can be raised and identify likely major donors, but will also flush out willing campaign leadership and highlight possible areas of concern. Ideally such a study should be conducted by external professionals so that it can be as objective as possible and confidential.

Reviewer's Comment

A feasibility study involves asking key individuals to review an organisation – its plans, its aims and its fundraising strategy. They could also be asked whether they might consider making a gift, if asked, and their motives for doing so or not. If undertaken by an impartial third party (usually a consultancy), the interviews are kept confidential and anonymous, but the exercise gives an idea of the attitudes of your targets and the likelihood of potential support.

Continues on next page

Matching the project with the individual donor's specific interests (his or her "hot button") is a particularly distinctive feature of successful fundraising planning. Much time needs to be spent working on this very issue prior to asking anyone for money. Further, the ultimate success of the fundraising programme will depend more on the thoroughness of this planning aspect than almost any other. If the commencement of asking needs to be delayed whilst donor research proceeds, then so be it.

Often in a discussion with potential donors, the project that the fundraisers want to pursue is sidelined for one that emerges as the item of real passion for the donor. It should be recognised that individual giving motivations may change the spending priorities of a board when suddenly funds become available for a project which might not have been near the top of its "wish list." This is generally acceptable provided the key strategic thrust of the organisation is not undermined in the process.

Good fundraising organisations are quick to recognise this and are ready with a range of projects at hand. This is not to say that a thoroughly researched and rational strategic plan should be overturned at the whim of a potential donor, but it does recognise that the various financial needs of an organisation can be accommodated by different giving motivations.

OPERATIONAL NEEDS

Many organisations depend on philanthropic support for significant elements of their operational expenses. The fundraising planning, therefore, needs to identify different types of programmes and tailor appropriate fundraising tools and techniques in response. Consideration should be given therefore to an "annual appeal" or "annual giving" programme which can be mounted in support of operational needs.

Annual giving sits comfortably alongside and is supportive of more substantial capital appeals. An annual appeal allows for a range of giving that may not be appropriate for capital appeals because the giving levels are too low. It may also allow for donors who would not ordinarily support bricks-and-mortar campaigns or other substantial fundraising efforts but who may want to be involved in ongoing projects which support the continued existence of the organisation.

Planning, especially as it relates to annual giving, should also recognise and allow for the various types of contributions from the corporate sector. These include "matched giving" where employers will match the gifts of their employees to certain organisations or causes within predetermined levels.

Reviewer's Comment

Additional ways of raising smaller amounts include organising sponsorship, selling branded merchandise, and marketing affinity products and services – for example holidays, credit cards, etc. Such goods are provided by the usual companies but are simply stamped with your organisation's name, for which you receive a portion of the profits. Income raised in these ways can be used to fund needs that might be less emotive or appealing to donors.

CAPITAL CAMPAIGNS, SCHOLARSHIPS AND OTHER FUNDS

Major capital appeals will generally focus on bricks and mortar or facility needs, but the planning should also recognize that many donors will want to give to scholarship funds, faculty programmes (possibly including named

chairs), sporting programmes and other funds created for specific purposes within an organisation.

Since capital appeals will be for large sums of money, they will focus on large donors and employ all the skills and strategies outlined in this Guide for dealing with them.

ENDOWMENT FUNDS

Apart from immediate budgetary needs and the organisation's capital wish list, prudent fundraising planning should take account of the need to ensure the long-term financial security of the organisation. Typically this will dictate the establishment and support of an endowment fund, which generally will not be tapped for recurrent or capital project purposes.

In planning for such a fund, attention will need to be given to those donors more likely to be attracted by such a concept, and fundraising tools such as bequest programmes will need to be researched and implemented.

It is worthwhile remembering that gifts to an endowment fund are likely to be fewer in number than those to

Continues on next page

annual giving campaigns or a capital appeal, but in quantum are likely to be far far greater.

Needs and Techniques

In the preceding sections, we have canvassed some fundraising needs and linked them with particular fundraising techniques. It is useful to summarise these and add some other techniques for which planning should take into account.

Need	Appropriate Techniques
Operational and minor capital costs	Annual giving and matched giving
Major capital projects	Capital appeals and major gifts
Scholarships and endowment	Bequests and other planned giving
Friend raising and minor fundraising	Special events

Giving Incentives and Thanking

"Find seven ways to thank your donors" is conventional fundraising wisdom. A simple letter of thanks (enclosing a receipt for taxation purposes if required) is obligatory, but it should be just the start of the thanking process. In preparing for fundraising, the honouring and thanking process for donors must be planned and approved ahead of asking. It should not be left until after the event.

The ways and means of thanking can be creative and will vary by organisation and by project, but the following graduated listing will serve as a guide:

- A thank-you letter signed by the CEO, foundation chair or the like.

- Mention of the donor's name in the listing of donors in the organisation's community magazine (but observing anonymity if requested).

- Invitations to functions held to honour donors.

- The seeking of advice from key donors as to upcoming projects and their funding.

- An invitation for certain donors to serve on advisory panels or committees.

- Recognition on plaques honouring those who gave to a particular project.

■ The offer of naming opportunities when the quantum of the gift justifies it.

Reviewer's Comment
In some countries, thank-you gifts may also be appropriate. Look at similar organisations to determine what is culturally and practically appropriate.

NAMING OPPORTUNITIES

These are typically associated with buildings, sporting facilities and other identifiable physical areas within organisations, but they can also be scholarship funds, professional staff-development programmes and endowment funds.

It may be traditional for an organisation to honour "doers," such as former heads of schools or former presidents of the board of directors, rather than "givers" when naming buildings, rooms and the like. Clearly a sensitive balance needs to be found between these two differing groups of organisational supporters so that the naming opportunity is not diminished in either group's eyes.

Reviewer's Comment
Further ideas include: creating honours/medals/special certificates, asking major donors to sign a "roll of benefactors", giving donors the opportunity to meet the beneficiaries of their generosity.

When seeking to maximise fundraising potential, the availability of naming opportunities can help an organisation in the following ways:

■ A new or upgraded building or facility may be funded in full.

■ The gift may raise the sights of other major prospects who will view the initial gift as a benchmark or standard for their own gift.

■ The association with a prominent individual, corporation or foundation may enhance the image of the organisation (the donor may also seek and receive some reciprocal association benefit).

■ A sufficiently large gift may generate positive publicity simply because of its size.

Continues on next page

OTHER THANK-YOU OPPORTUNITIES

Equal thought should be expended on all thank-you opportunities which are used either as incentives to give or as rewards for giving.

It is imperative that all thank-you opportunities be properly executed. For example, inclusion of a supporter in lists of donors or on plaques (either real or virtual ones online) is an area that can be particularly fraught with danger. Misspelling a name, inclusion in a wrong category or omission from a list can cause untold damage to a relationship that has taken months or years to establish. Too much or too little recognition for donations also can damage relationships.

Think carefully about what is provided to donors by similar organisations. Think creatively but within the context of cultural, financial and organisational considerations.

STAFFING AND OTHER RESOURCES

Ideally, the Board will delegate the management of high value fundraising within an organisation to a group selected for their philanthropic experience or intent. Such a group, comprising volunteers and select senior organisational management (including the Chief Executive Officer), might be titled the "Foundation Board" or some similar name. A title along the lines of "Fundraising Committee" does not sufficiently portray the seriousness of the task either for the organisation or for the individuals sitting on that committee.

Reviewer's Comment
Foundation boards should be seen as prestigious and an honour to join.

In serious philanthropy, leadership, both organisational and financial, is all-important. If campaign leadership and potential lead donors to the organisation consider 1,000 to be a substantial gift, then that will set the tone for the whole campaign. Conversely, if the lead gift is 50,000, 100,000 or 500,000, then that too, will provide the path for others to follow. The net result on the outcome of a campaign is considerable.

Those sitting on the Foundation Board must therefore be thinking in substantial terms if they are to have the positive impact that is called for. Critically they:

- Must not be afraid to aim high.
- Must be prepared to make their own early gift to the extent that their circumstances allow.
- Must be prepared to ask others to give to the extent that their circumstances allow.

Reviewer's Comment
In some countries, it is customary for anyone sitting on such a board to make a gift as part of his or her position.

Representation on such a board from across the organisation's constituency is also important: older and younger constituents, males and females, alumni, staff and board members. Balance and appropriate representation are all-important if the organisation wishes to successfully tap its various constituencies.

Continues on next page

STAFFING AND OTHER RESOURCES

The CEO (or director or whatever the staff person in charge is called) is usually the best person to espouse the vision that dictates the fundraising needs of the organisation. His or her role is vital in helping to engage potential donors with the expression of the organisation's vision. In most cases, however, it is inappropriate for the CEO to make the actual ask (this is best left to influential volunteers or the Director of Development), but the CEO should be part of the team, especially with key donors.

Reviewer's Comment
In some countries, the CEO or head staff person would be seen as the person to make the ask. It is important to find out what is appropriate in your area.

Remembering that the most influential and high level asking will be done by committed volunteers who themselves have given, a Director of Development (sometimes known as the Director of Fundraising) can be most effective by:

- Commissioning ongoing in-depth donor research.

- Orchestrating proactive donor cultivation.

- Organising and stage-managing the asking process.

- Overseeing a creative, segmented annual giving programme designed to bring forward future major donors.

- Ensuring that the bequest/legacy message is heard in a discreet but continuing manner.

To operate effectively, the Director of Development must work out of presentable quarters, recognising that a positive and authoritative profile needs to be projected to potential donors. This will generally mean that he or she will be adjacent to the "front door" of the organisation same as the CEO. Proximity to the CEO should also be considered an important factor if the Director of Development is to be effective in the public relations/donor cultivation role.

STAFFING AND OTHER RESOURCES

It is important that the Development Office is part of senior management in order to give it credibility and to demonstrate that it is a central part of the organisation and is delivering the organisation's objectives.

Type of office, physical location and precise details relating to the terms of employment will vary depending on the type of organisation, country of the organisation and culture within which the organisation works.

Provision of appropriate computer hardware and software is obligatory if the process of donor research, from friend raising to fundraising, is to be achieved. Integration of the records of the development office via one of the now available integrated organisational administration software packages is highly desirable.

It is important to have administrative support, because an ongoing task of the development function is to collect and maintain accurate data. Also, it is important to ensure that information on your constituencies is located, or at least rationalised, in a single database to avoid confusion and duplication – a common challenge in universities, for example, is that information on students and information on alumni are often stored on different databases within totally separate departments.

Secretarial support, perhaps part-time at the outset, is vital if the development function is to achieve its goals. It may well be that it is most critical in the early stages as the highly labour-intensive task of establishing a reliable database proceeds.

Reporting relationships as well as opportunities for adequate communication are vital given the involvement of the Director of Development with senior and potentially influential members of the organisation's community. This implies

Continues on next page

that the Director of Development should report directly to the CEO and that he or she should have at least observer status at the board table. Major donors will want to deal with someone who has demonstrable and appropriate status.

A good rule of thumb is that an effective development/fundraising office (if involved in fundraising on a full-time basis), should be generating revenue that is five times the amount of the direct costs of the office after no more than five years from a standing start. This excludes receipts from bequests and legacies, which cannot be budgeted for with any certainty. The key variables which will impact on this include the age and socioeconomic status of the organisation, the extent to which fundraising is pursued by the development office to the exclusion of other activities such as marketing, and the support given to the function by the CEO and the board.

In general terms, it needs to be recognised that fundraising is a long-term process and success is most likely to result from the careful nurturing of relationships, which cannot be achieved overnight. In the long run, if it is the financial security of the organisation which is at stake, then time spent on getting the process right will be a sound investment.

If the key players in the development office have little or no experience in conducting serious philanthropy, then they need appropriate training. The earlier in the process this is done, preferably by outside and objective professionals, the sooner that asking with confidence can begin and results obtained.

This training should comprise two components, designed to be mutually supportive:

■ An overview of fundraising processes, donor giving motivation, giving incentives such as naming opportunities, relevant taxation considerations, and a history of philanthropy within the organisation.

■ An understanding of presentation skills, one-on-one solicitation techniques, non-verbal response messages, and participation in individualised and relevant role-play.

Such training will equip volunteers and organisational management with the skills, and importantly the confidence, to solicit and obtain substantial gifts.

ORGANISATIONAL SIZE CONSIDERATIONS

Planning to engage in serious fundraising requires that organisations consider how far their budgets will extend, what resources should be applied, what the likely returns are for a given level of investment, and to what extent their organisation will benefit at the end of the day. Smaller organisations will also be critically aware that competition for the philanthropic dollar is becoming more intense by the day, and they will want to know how they can elbow their way in and secure their share.

These questions will weigh especially heavily on smaller organisations with limited resources, and they in particular should pay attention to size-related planning strategies:

- Gifts-in-kind (gifts of products or provision of staff time by companies) in the early days of establishing a philanthropic programme can be of immense value.

- Some farsighted donors see merit in funding the establishment of a development function within an organisation so that it can have a catalytic effect and bring forward other early donors.

- Volunteers can play a vital role in establishing a programme, paving the way for paid development staff to follow at a later time.

- Development employees need not be full-time at the outset, and often, relevant skills can be found within those already involved with the organisation (for example, the parent body of a school or directors of an organisation).

Creativity is all-important as smaller organisations seek to make an initial investment in the process of philanthropy, but even the smallest organisation will be doing itself a disservice if it does not provide a climate and setting whereby its constituents can support it financially.

The increasing international mobility of alumni of schools and universities and supporters of a whole range of other causes means that organisations worldwide are paying ever more attention to international fundraising. Two common characteristics tend to emerge which need to be factored into planning for the international segment of a constituency:

■ Potential supporters living far away from their alma mater or other organisation of interest are often more passionate about and supportive of that organisation than those who reside "around the corner".

■ Maintaining current addresses and, more particularly, recovering lost addresses internationally, brings with it a level of complexity which is not found in the "national" scene.

Reviewer's Comment
If potential supporters are located far away from the physical base of the organisation, you should explore ways of creating a local 'presence' e.g. through a website, newsletters and events.

The planning process needs to recognise both the potential and the maintenance associated with servicing international members of the constituency, but on balance organisations generally find the benefits outweigh the costs.

Strategies, which should be factored into the planning at an early time, include the recruitment of overseas agents or representatives by country from amongst the international constituents, and an "inclusive" approach when distributing organisational literature and conducting reunion programmes or special events for donors.

TAX ISSUES

Within this overview of preparing for fundraising, space does not allow for anything approaching a comprehensive view of national and international tax considerations and how they might benefit the donor and/or the organisation. What needs to be recognised during planning for obtaining gifts, however, is that tax benefits can be a key giving motivation for donors and they need to be maximised to the extent that the law allows.

Whilst some surveys of giving motivation amongst donors suggest that access to tax benefits is not a high-ranking factor, the absence of it, when it is offered by competing organisations, is quite likely to deny the organisation a gift. This is particularly so in countries where the tax benefits are substantial enough to be worth having.

Part of the fundraising planning process, therefore, must include a creative review of taxation measures available to likely supporters of the organisation, both nationally and internationally. In most countries, the opportunities for national taxation benefits are relatively transparent, but it should be noted that there is much movement on the international front (a donor resident in one country giving to an organisation resident in another), and careful research is required where an organisation has international elements in its constituency.

Donors invariably like to "get on board" with organisations that have a clear and unambiguous strategic plan and which exhibit present or potential success stories in their fundraising endeavours. Successful fundraising, therefore, tends to reside in those organisations which plan well, which effectively communicate their planning with passion and style to their constituencies, and which project a strong "corporate" image.

Organisations which fundraise successfully typically pay close attention to whether they and their community are ready for a serious campaign. In determining if they are in a "go" situation or a "no-go" situation, regard will be given to:

- The status of friend raising preparatory to fundraising.

- The level of key donor cultivation which has occurred.

- The availability of influential volunteer askers who themselves have given or will give in a substantial way.

- The presence of a well-thought-through strategic plan inclusive of the projects in question.

- The availability of a well-researched and board-adopted policy on naming opportunities both for physical facilities and for specific programmes such as scholarships.

- The availability of appropriate tax benefits for donors.

- The presence of, or the ability to quickly implement, support for the fundraising activity via a development function.

Generally an organisation is well-advised to delay the launch of a major campaign until most, if not all, of these key measures of readiness are in place. Whilst this could delay a significant fundraising programme for six or even 12 months is it generally prudent to do so in the knowledge that more comprehensive planning will help ensure success.

CONCLUSION

An examination of the history of a whole range of nonprofit organisations in a range of countries suggests that philanthropy generally was there at the outset in one form or another. It is a truism that it is never too soon to start.

Programmes need not be grandiose or sophisticated at the beginning, but the sooner constituents come to understand that philanthropy is part of the equation, the sooner the organisation will be equipped to fulfil its mission. Philanthropy is often spoken of as being a continuum. In the school setting, for example, an old cap donated to the archives today turns into a modest gift to the annual fund tomorrow, which eventually leads to a major gift for a building, and ultimately the school is remembered in the donor's estate!

Start modestly certainly, but start!

AUTHOR

FRANK OPRAY, AUTHOR

Frank Opray, has ten years experience as Director of Development firstly at Wesley College Melbourne and subsequently at Carey Grammar School Melbourne.

Prior to these appointments he spent many years in finance, market research and in management consulting, primarily in the services sector. During that time he was for three years a Council member and Treasurer of Wesley College Melbourne, Australia's largest school with over 3,600 students.

In recognition of his work in fundraising and marketing at Wesley and for the Development profession, Frank received the inaugural award of *"Fundraiser of the Year"* at the 1992 joint conference of the Australian Institute of Fundraising and the Association of Development and Alumni Professionals in Education, (ADAPE).

Frank Opray holds a B.Com from The University of Melbourne and is a qualified accountant. He volunteers his time as President of the Queen's College Foundation, University of Melbourne, as President of the Old Wesley Collegians' Association Melbourne, and as Honorary Secretary in Australasia and Asia for the British Schools and Universities Foundation Inc, New York. He is a Fellow of ADAPE and was its founding Secretary/Treasurer.

Frank regularly presents papers at educational conferences in Australia, in Asia and in Europe.

Alison Woolley, Reviewer

Alison Woolley is a Senior Development Manager at UCL (University College London) with particular responsibility for UCL's development programme in the U.S. Alison has built up a network of key supporters there, and manages relationships with foundations and individual donors.

She is also involved in developing projects and proposals in conjunction with academics at the university in London, and has raised money for these closer to home. Prior to joining UCL, she worked in alumni relations and fundraising at Bristol University for 4 years, where she was responsible for various activities, including bringing in major gifts to build an indoor sports centre and for a number of academic initiatives.